20 Quick & Easy Knitting Projects

SPRING HOUSE PRESS

Contents

20

Cozy Classic Pillow

22

Cozy Classic Blanket

24

Garter Stitch Scarf

26

Double Knit Scarf

30

Kid's One Zippy Scarf

32

Seed Stitch Scarf

34

Simple Hat

36

Soft Smiles Hat

38

Zippy Classic Hat and Scarf

40

Blanket Jacket

43

Sweet Savannah Blanket

46

Cozy Rug

48

Little Apple Hat

50

Magical Stitch Blanket

52

Sweet Savannah Blanket

54

Braided Pillow

57

Cable Cowl Wristers

60

Faux Cable Foot Stool

65

Rain Dance Shawl

68

Hooded Super Scarf

Getting Started with Zippy Loom

Welcome to super-fast knitting with Zippy Loom! You will be able to make many different items with the Zippy configurations. Make hats, scarves, blankets, shawls, and so much more, very quickly and easily. Fun for all!

This book contains 20 patterns from basic beginner patterns to more elaborate large projects using many Zippy Looms and Connectors. Start with some super-simple scarves knit with 1 or 2 Zippys, and then, just keep going . . . learn to make big blankets using 12 Zippy Looms and Zippy Corners. The project possibilities are endless, and there is something for all knitters, from beginner to advanced.

Zippy Looms are modular looms that can be attached together with the different connectors to form longer looms, square looms, rectangular looms, and double knit looms. By using corners and "L" pieces, you can create different size looms.

Zippy Loom Parts

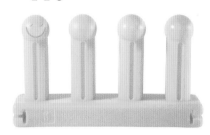

Zippy Loom

Corner

Straight Connector

"L" Connector   Regular Connector

Zippy Configurations

Patterns, in this book, work with 10 different Zippy configurations. Here are some basic setups with diagrams, showing how the looms are attached.

4 Zippy Looms + 4 Zippy Corners

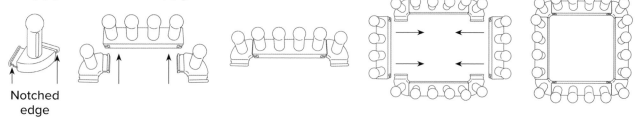

Notched edge

4 Zippy Looms + 4 "L" Connectors

Notched edge

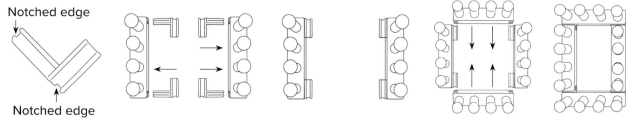

Notched edge

4 Zippy Looms attached with 2 Straight Connectors

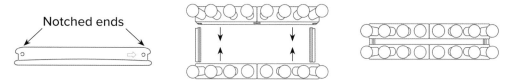

Notched ends

2 Zippy Looms connected with 1 Regular Connector

Pattern Basics

Yarn Weight

Zippy Looms work best with super-bulky yarns, #6 or #7. You can also use 2 strands of thinner yarns to create thickness. For novel effects, try ruffle or fancy yarns.

Difficulty Ratings

You will see difficulty ratings on each project. They rank from one zippy face (the easiest) 😊 😊 😊 😊 😊 to five (more difficult) 😊 😊 😊 😊 😊 .

As you read each pattern, you will discover abbreviations and symbols.

Pattern Abbreviations

approx = approximately

c1 over 2 left = cable 1 over 2 left

c1 over 2 right = cable 1 over 2 right

CA = color A

CB = color B

CC = color C

CD = color D

CO = cast on

ek = e-wrap knit stitch

k = knit stitch

KO = knit off

LT = left twist

LTP = left twist purl

p = purl stitch

rep = repeat

rnd(s) = round(s)

RT = right twist

RTP = right twist purl

s1 = slip 1 stitch

sl1wyb = skip with yarn to back

st(s) = stitch(es)

W&T = wrap and turn

WY = working yarn

Reading Pattern Symbols

Remember the meanings of the following symbols, which will appear between other terms and abbreviations to indicate actions:

An asterisk (*): Placed before an instruction that should be repeated.

A comma (,): Separates two different steps in the knitting pattern.

Brackets [ ] / Parentheses ( ): Indicate a section of the instruction to be repeated a certain number of times.

Reading Charts

Charts are visual representations of the stitch pattern from the right side of the pattern. Many knitters prefer knitting from a chart as it allows them to see the stitch pattern ahead of time, identify areas of potential errors, and rectify them before embarking on the project.

Every chart should contain a key. The key or legend helps identify the symbols. Each symbol represents a stitch or a set of stitches. Interpreting the key/legend is crucial to create the finished item. As you see the chart, you will note that it is made of tiny squares. Each square represents a stitch. Charts typically have all rows/rounds shown; if the designer omitted the wrong side rows/rounds, the pattern will indicate this omission. On the chart, you will also see numbers on the sides. If the stitch pattern is to be worked in rows, the chart will have numbers on both the right and left side. If the stitch pattern is to be worked in the round, the chart will have numbers on the right side only.

Once you know the stitch pattern's key and whether it is worked in rows or rounds, you are ready to begin knitting from the chart.

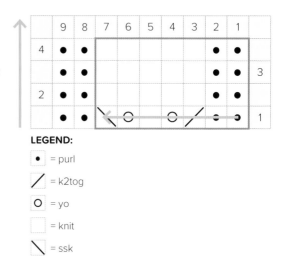

LEGEND:

• = purl

／ = k2tog

O = yo

☐ = knit

＼ = ssk

Right side rows: Read the chart from right to left and from bottom to top. The second row is read from left to right.

Wrong side rows (even numbers): These are read from left to right.

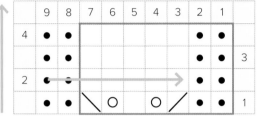

LEGEND:

• = purl

╱ = k2tog

○ = yo

☐ = knit

╲ = ssk

Pattern repeats: Heavy lines in the chart indicate stitch pattern repeats. After the heavy line, the chart indicates the edge stitches that are located at the end of the row.

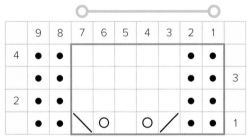

LEGEND:

• = purl

╱ = k2tog

○ = yo

☐ = knit

╲ = ssk

Understanding Knitting Gauge

Knitting gauge is the number of stitches per inch you create on your loom, and number of rows per inch as you work the length vertically. Most patterns will tell you the target gauge. You can determine gauge by knitting a small swatch (a small square of knitting, usually about 10 to 12 stitches, and 10 to 12 rows) and measuring its dimensions. You may want to measure based on 2 or 3" (5 or 8cm) in order to come up with whole numbers. (Example: 7 sts x 9 rows = 2" [5cm])

By knowing the gauge you will be knitting, you will be able to make adjustments to size by simply adding the correct number of stitches for each additional inch of width, or the correct number of rows for additional length.

Blocking Your Knits

When you take your knitting off the loom, it is a good idea to block your stitches. Blocking evens out your stitches, relaxes the yarn, and allows you to adjust the sizing. You will have a more polished, finished look to your garment. After knitting a garment or a section, it has tendencies to draw tighter and curl on some of the edges, and be just a bit out of shape.

Note: Acrylic yarn cannot be blocked.

The technique of blocking each knitted piece will result in a more professional and properly finished piece. It will also help when joining the pieces together, such as a sweater or afghan that was knit in sections. Blocking helps to set the shape of the piece so that it responds as it was knitted and won't be pulled out of shape, as this will create an ill-fitted garment. This is also true if you have designs in the knit.

Needed items: Rust-proof pins, a spray bottle of purified water, and a large flat area.

It is important to have a base for the knit that is large enough for the piece to be fully laid out. This can be an ironing board or a bed with tight-fitting cover or sheet, or the floor with towels for very large pieces (yoga mats work well for this).

1 Lay the item flat on the base so that the knit is positioned to correct gauge and size of knitting.

2 Hold the piece in place with the no-rust pins. Be sure to use enough pins so that all edges are held in place securely.

3 Spray the knit with water from the spray bottle so that the knit is damp to touch. Allow piece to remain pinned until fully dry.

4 When the piece is fully dry, the pins can be removed and it will remain flat. Shake the piece slightly to fluff the yarn back to original loftiness. The piece is now ready to be joined to the rest of the garment, once all pieces are blocked.

Note: Item must be blocked again after every washing.

Yarn

When using the Zippy Loom, it is recommended to use super-bulky (#6) or jumbo yarn (#7), or 2 strands of bulky or super-bulky (#5 or #6) yarn. For creating a novel effect, try a ruffle, boucle, or a fabric yarn. Working with all these different yarns is just fun to see the results.

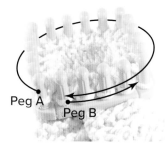

Peg A
Peg B

Knitting in Flat Panels

Flat panels are used in scarves, shawls, blankets, and even to create parts for sweaters! With panels, the knit is worked in rows: one direction is row 1 and returning in the opposite direction is row 2.

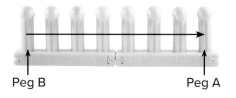

Peg B   Peg A

When knitting a flat panel, work back and forth from one end of the loom to the other end, and then reverse the direction. The first row goes from right to left, (clockwise); so, in order to have the correct setup for the first row, you will begin your cast on at the last peg, peg B. Then, the first row of pattern will start with peg A.

Cast on from B to A. Work the first row from peg A to peg B. This can be done using Zippys in a straight configuration or in a round configuration.

When knitting a flat panel with a round configuration, work starting from peg A, and continue all the way around the loom to the last peg, B. Then reverse and knit back to starting peg. Do this without connecting the first and last stitches. Continue in this method. Notice there will no connection between beginning peg A and last peg B.

Knitting in the Round

You can also use the Zippy Loom for knitting in the round, such as for hats, cowls, leg warmers, and anything tubular.

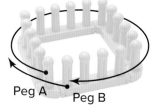

Peg A   Peg B

When knitting in the round, start working from peg A and continue all the way around the loom to last peg, B. Then continue in the same direction around the loom, again starting with beginning peg A. It is continuous. Peg A is connected to peg B.

Cast Ons

Casting on is the process of putting the first row of yarn on your loom.

E-Wrap Cast On

1 Make a loop with the yarn. Reach inside the circle (loop), grab the working yarn, and pass it through the circle to form a slipknot.

2 Place this slipknot on the first peg.

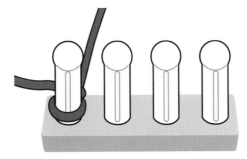

3 Moving from left to right on the loom, wrap the working yarn around the 2nd peg. Wrap the pegs in a clockwise direction.

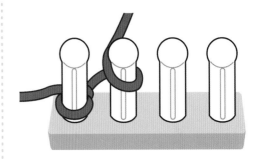

4 Repeat with the remaining pegs until all pegs are cast on. You are now ready to work in a stitch pattern for the first row or first round.

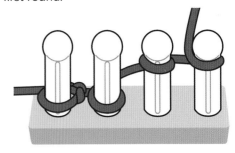

Tip: Hold on to the yarn. Once you have wrapped that last peg, the yarn may unwind if you let go.

Crochet Cast On

1 Create slipknot.

2 Place slipknot on first peg. Insert crochet hook through the slipknot. Take working yarn to the inside of the knitting loom.

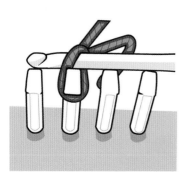

3 Grab working yarn with the crochet hook.

4 Pull through the loop on the peg.

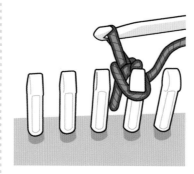

5 Place on next empty peg. Repeat process until all pegs are cast on.

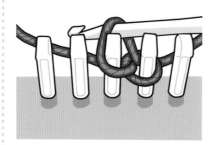

Stitches

E-Wrap Stitch (ek)

1 This is worked like the e-wrap cast on. Wrap around each peg in an e-motion counterclockwise with the yarn. E-wrap every peg. **Note:** The first peg will be wrapped in the same direction as the previous row.

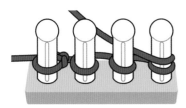

2 Reverse direction of the wrap with the remaining pegs.

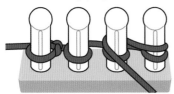

3 Each peg should now have 2 loops. Lift the bottom loop off the peg. Let it fall toward the inside of the knitting loom.

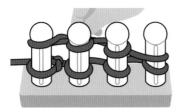

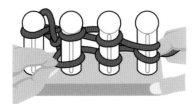

Tip: To prevent your yarn from coming off the pegs, hook over the last peg wrapped; do this first. This will anchor the wraps in place while you work the remaining pegs.

Knit Stitch (k)

In loom knitting, the knit stitch has a few more steps than the e-wrap stitch. When completed, these steps form a stitch that looks identical to the knit stitch created on knitting needles.

1 Place the working yarn in front of the peg, above the loop on the peg. Insert the knit hook under the loop on the peg from the bottom up.

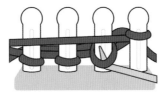

2 Reach up to catch the working yarn with the hook. Pull the working yarn down through the loop on the peg, forming a new loop.

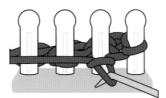

3 Pull the loop that is still on the peg up and off the peg.

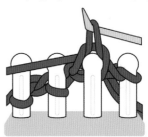

4 Place the new loop that is on the hook, onto the peg. Gently pull on the working yarn to tighten the stitch.

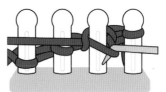

Repeat steps 1–4.

U Stitch (u)

The U stitch is similar to the knit stitch, but creates a tighter stitch.

Bring yarn to the front of the peg, wrap around the peg to the back of the loom, then hook over or work the peg. Wrapping yarn around the peg forces the yarn to remain loose while knitting.

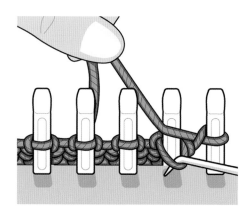

Purl Stitch (p)

This stitch is the reverse of the knit stitch.

1 Place the working yarn in front of the peg, below the loop on the peg. Insert the knit hook under the loop on the peg from the top down.

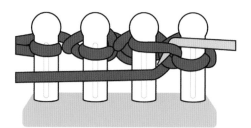

2 Reach down to catch the working yarn with the knit hook. Pull the working yarn up through the loop on the peg, forming a new loop. Hold that loop.

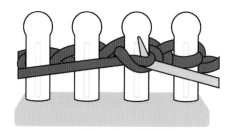

3 Then, pull the loop that is still on the peg up and off the peg.

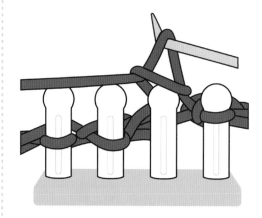

4 Place the new loop onto the peg. Gently tug on the working yarn to tighten the stitch.

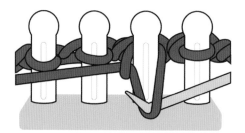

Cables

Cables Over 2 Stitches

This creates a rope-like twist in your knitting. These can be worked over several stitches. A cable needle or a stitch holder will be helpful.

LEFT CROSSING (LC-2 STITCHES)

1 Take working yarn behind peg 1; skip this peg.

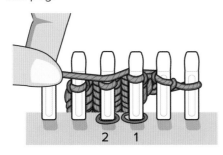

2 Knit peg 2, and then place on a cable needle.

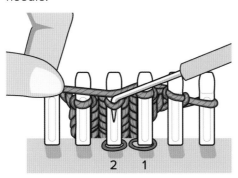

3 Move stitch on peg 1 to peg 2.

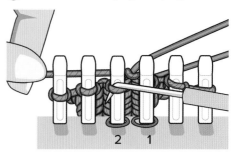

4 Place stitch from cable needle onto peg 1.

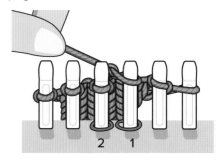

5 Knit peg 2.

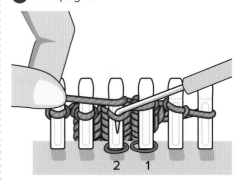

RIGHT CROSSING (RC-2 STITCHES)

1 Place stitch 1 on a cable needle and hold to center of loom.

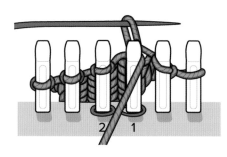

4 Take stitch off cable needle and place on peg 2.

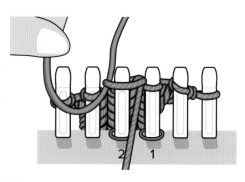

2 Move yarn to front of peg 2 and knit the peg.

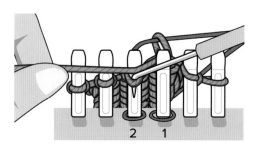

5 Knit peg 2.

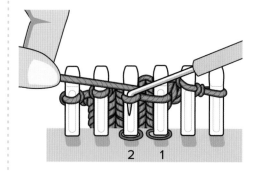

3 Move this stitch from peg 2 to peg 1.

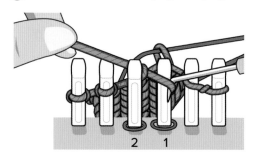

Finishing Techniques

Basic Bind Off

When your knitting is complete, you are ready to remove knit from the loom (binding off your stitches).

1 Knit the first 2 stitches (peg 1 and peg 2).

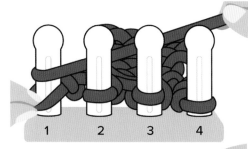

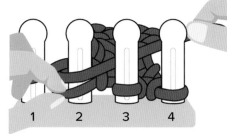

2 Next, move the loop from peg 2 over to peg 1. Lift the bottom loop up and off the peg. 1.

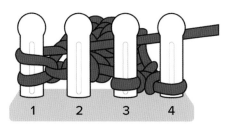

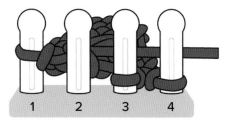

3 Move the remaining loop from peg 1 to peg 2. Peg 1 is now empty (you have bound off one stitch).

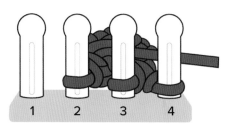

4 Repeat this process. Take working yarn to front of peg 3; work peg 3 by taking the bottom loop up and over the peg. Move loop from peg 3 to peg 2. Lift bottom loop off peg 2. Move loop from peg 2 to peg 3. Continue in this process until last stitch remains. Cut working yarn. Bring the yarn tail through the last loop on the loom to finish. Weave in all ends.

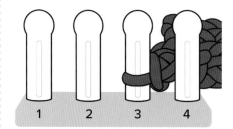

Gather Bind Off for Hats

This technique is used in removing hats from the loom. Cut the working yarn coming from the hat, leaving a 16 to 20" (40 to 51cm) tail for the gathering process.

1 Use a large darning needle (in illustration) or fingers to remove loops from loom. Skip the first 2 pegs, and remove the stitches from the next 2 pegs and place on yarn tail.

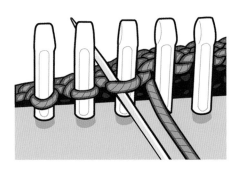

2 Continue process of skipping 2 pegs and picking up 2 stitches until you reach the end of the round. Go around the loom again, removing the remaining stitches.

3 Cinch the top closed. Weave ends in.

Mattress Stitch

The mattress stitch is a seaming technique that creates an invisible edge on the front of your knitting.

Lay pieces down on a flat surface, right side up. Insert a tapestry needle under the horizontal stitch that connects each edge stitch. Pull yarn through and insert the needle under this horizontal stitch on the opposite knit piece. Continue working back and forth in the same process. After several stitches, gently pull the pieces together. Then, repeat until seam is complete (best to use matching color yarn).

Weaving In Ends

After your knit is complete, you will want to hide your ends on the back side.

1 Pull ends to back side.

2 With a crochet hook, pull through the purl stitches in a zigzag pattern.

3 Continue for about 1" (3cm) and then cut. If the end is at a seam, simply pull into seam.

Cozy Classic Pillow

 Size: 16 x 14" (41 x 36cm) | **Gauge:** 4 sts x 8 rows = 4" (10cm) stockinette stitch

This stylish and chunky pillow will look at home in any décor. Customize it with some funky or classic buttons! It's a great addition to any sofa and looks fantastic with the Classic Blanket.

Instructions:

CO 16 sts; prepare to work a flat panel. (Make 2.)

Rows 1–30: K4, p8, k4.

Bind off using Basic Bind Off method (page 17).

Block lightly (page 9).

Attaching Panels

1 First, using a whipstitch, sew 2 finished panels together on 3 sides with wrong sides facing outward.

2 Turn the sewn panels inside-out so right side is now outward-facing.

3 Stuff pillow using quilted batting (or preferred stuffing material).

4 Sew remaining opening together, thus enclosing the batting in the pillow.

5 Sew on buttons, pom-poms, or bows as desired.

What's Needed:

Knitting Loom: 4 Zippy Looms, 16 pegs total.

Yarn: Approx 82 yds (75m) super-bulky or jumbo yarn. (Sample uses Patons Cobbles in Winter White.)

   6 SUPER BULKY **or** **7** JUMBO

Notions: Knitting tool, tapestry needle, scissors, large decorative buttons, preferred material to stuff pillow (approximately 14 x 110" [36 x 279 cm] quilt batting used in sample).

Cozy Classic Blanket

☺ ☺ ☺ ☺ ☺ | **Size:** 48 x 70 (122 x 178cm) | **Gauge:** 4 sts x 8 rows = 4" (10cm) stockinette stitch

This great beginner pattern will be your "cozy" go-to blanket on those chilly winter evenings.

Instructions:

Panel 1
CO 16 sts; prepare to work a flat panel.

Row 1: K16.

Row 2: P16.

Rows 3–6: [Row 1–2] 2x.

Row 7: K12, [p1, k1] 2x.

Row 8: [K1, p1] 2x, k12.

Rep rows 7–8, 68 times.

Row 145: P16.

Row 146: K16.

Rep rows 145–146, 2 times.

Bind off using Basic Bind Off (page 17).

Block lightly (page 9).

Panel 2
CO 16 sts; prepare to work a flat panel.

Row 1: K16.

Row 2: P16.

Rows 3–6: [Rows 1–2] 2x.

Rows 7–144: P16.

Row 145: P16.

Row 146: K16.

Rep rows 145–146, 2 times.

Bind off using Basic Bind Off (page 17).

Block lightly (page 9).

Panel 3
CO 16 sts; prepare to work a flat panel.

Row 1: K16.

Row 2: P16.

Rows 3–6: [Rows 1–2] 2x.

Row 7: [K1, p1] 2x, k12.

Row 8: K12, [p1, k1] 2x.

Rep rows 7–8, 68 times.

Row 145: P16.

Row 146: K16.

Rep rows 145–146, 2 times.

Bind off using Basic Bind Off method (page 17).

Block lightly (page 9).

Using the mattress stitch (page 19), attach panel 1 to panel 2. Then, also using the mattress stitch, attach panel 2 to panel 3.

What's Needed:

Knitting Loom: 4 Zippy Looms, 16 pegs total

Yarn: Approx 615 yds (562m) super-bulky or jumbo yarn. (Sample uses Patons Cobbles in Winter White.)

 or
SUPER BULKY   JUMBO

Notions: Knitting tool, tapestry needle, scissors.

Pattern Notes:

This pattern is composed of 3 individual panels that are sewn together. Make each panel separately and sew together as per instructions.

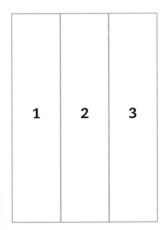

Garter Stitch Scarf

⊙⊙⊙⊙⊙ | **Size:** 6 x 40" (15 x 102cm) | **Gauge:** 4 sts = 4" (10cm)

We love this stitch with Zippy Loom. It knits up in a jiffy, but makes quite a look that is smashing in a short version or in a full-length super scarf. Get started with Zippy with this Garter Stitch Scarf. It is so fast to knit—you might as well knit one in all your favorite fall colors.

What's Needed:

Knitting Loom: 2 Zippy Looms, 8 pegs total

Yarn: 1 skein (approx 49 yds [45m]) super-bulky or jumbo yarn. (Samples use Loops & Threads, Chunky Braid; and Loops & Threads, Ziggy, both colors discontinued.)

  or

Notions: Knitting tool, crochet hook, scissors.

Instructions:

Assemble 2 Zippy Looms together. CO 8 sts and prepare to work a flat panel.

Row 1: Ek to end.

Row 2: P to end.

Rep 2 rows until 12" (30cm) of yarn left, or desired length.

Bind off with Basic Bind Off method (page 17).

Weave ends in (page 19). Your scarf is complete!

Double Knit Scarf

😊 😊 😊 😊 😊 | **Size:** 6 x 72" (15 x 183cm) | **Gauge:** 6 sts x 6 rows = 4" (10cm)

Create a scarf with lots of texture. The thick and thin yarn is super great in the double knit. You don't need to vary the stitch; just knit in the basic stitch to create a fantastic look. Two versions are photographed to show options. Try many different thick yarns for different looks.

What's Needed:

Knitting Loom: 4 Zippy Looms + 2 Straight Connectors + 2 Regular Connectors, 16 pegs total

Yarn: 1 skein (approx 69 yds [63m]) super-bulky or jumbo yarn. (Sample Rainbow Scarf uses Isaac Mizrahi CRAFT Lexington in Stuyvesant; Blue Skies uses Buttercream Thick and Thin in Blue.)

 SUPER BULKY or **JUMBO**

Notions: Knitting tool, tapestry needle, crochet hook.

Instructions:

1 CO 8 sts. Begin with a slipknot and place on first peg on back of loom. Weave around pegs, wrapping every other peg.

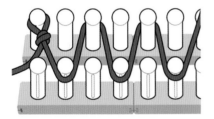

2 When you get to the end of the loom, or working section, bring yarn straight across at end and turn loom around and weave back, wrapping around the pegs that you skipped the first time.

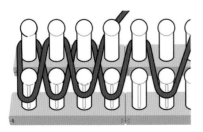

3 Set anchor yarn to secure the sts and assist with moving the first few rows. The anchor yarn is a scrap piece of yarn about 3 times the length of your sts. Lay it across the sts only. Allow anchor yarn to drop below the loom.

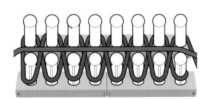

4 Rep the wrapping process over the anchor yarn until you have 2 loops on each peg.

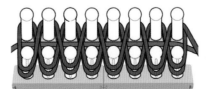

Double Knit Scarf

5 Hook over, bottom loop over top loop, on both sides of the loom. Your sts are now cast on. Pull down gently on the anchor yarn to secure the cast-on sts. Leave anchor yarn in knitting as you work.

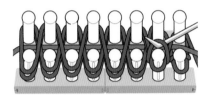

Row 1: Work in Stockinette stitch. Continue weave pattern as used in the cast on.

Turn your loom around; bring yarn around both end pegs, and continue to weave the open pegs.

Rep row 1 until approx 15" (38cm) of yarn remains.

> **Note:** You will still be weaving in an every-other-peg pattern. Hook over all pegs on the row.

1 Work from end opposite the yarn tail; use your crochet hook to lift off the first 2 loops, one from each side of the loom.

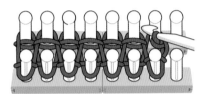

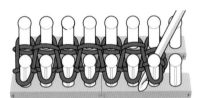

2 Pull 1 through 1. Then pick up next loop. Continue to end, always picking up from alternating sides of loom. Secure final stitch by pulling yarn tail through last loop on hook. With crochet hook, pull yarn tail into finished knit. Now your piece of double knit is off the loom.

> **Note:** When hooking over, work from the side edges inward, left end to center, and right end to center. This will keep the edges more even.

Bind off at anchor yarn.

The bind off puts a nice finished edge on your cast on stitches and allows the removal of the anchor yarn.

1 Start at end opposite the yarn tail. Use your crochet hook. Slip the first 2 loops onto crochet hook.

2 Pull loop closest to hook through the other loop. Continue to end by picking up each additional loop. When you have the last loop on crochet hook, pull the yarn tail through the last loop for knot. Tuck the yarn tail into the finished knit with crochet hook. Carefully remove anchor yarn from knitwear, and your knitted piece is complete. There is no need to block the piece with double knit.

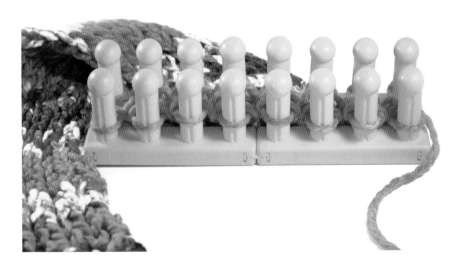

Kid's One-Zippy Scarf

 | **Size:** 3 x 40" (8 x 102cm) | **Gauge:** 4 sts = 4" (10cm)

Zippy's big pegs makes knitting ideal for kids...this is only a 20-minute project. Pick a colorful shade of yarn to craft this loveable scarf. Add pompoms or tassels to the ends for even more fun!

What's Needed:

Knitting Loom: 1 Zippy Loom, 4 pegs total

Yarn: 1 skein super-bulky or jumbo yarn.

 or

Notions: Knitting tool, crochet hook, scissors.

Instructions:

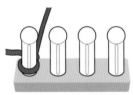

To CO, place the slipknot on the first peg on the left of the Zippy Loom.

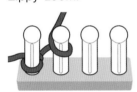

Moving from left to right, wrap the working yarn around 2nd peg in clockwise direction.

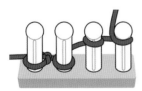

Rep with the remaining pegs.

Row 1: Ek to end.

Rep row 1 until scarf is as long as desired.

Bind off with Basic Bind Off method (page 17).

Weave in ends (page 9).

> **Option:** You can sew on pompoms for a fun look!

Seed Stitch Scarf

● ○ ○ ○ ○ | **Size:** 5 x 27½" (13 x 70cm) | **Gauge:** 6 sts x 7 rows = 4" (10cm)

This yummy scarf stands out in a crowd, and is so easy to knit up. It's created with the seed stitch pattern—a combination of the e-wrap and purl stitches—for lots of texture. Use a variegated yarn to give the stripe effect. Knit lots in your favorite colors!

What's Needed:

Knitting Loom: 2 Zippy Looms, 8 pegs total

Yarn: 1 skein (approx 69 yds [63m]) super-bulky or jumbo yarn. (Samples use Isaac Mizrahi CRAFT Lexington in Irving; and Red Heart Grande in Foggy.)

 or

Notions: Knitting tool, crochet hook, scissors.

Instructions:

Assemble 2 Zippy Looms together. CO 8 sts and prepare to work a flat panel.

Rows 1–3: Ek to end.

***Next 6 rows:** P to end.

Next 6 rows: Ek to end.*

Rep from * to * until about 2 feet (61cm) of yarn remain.

Last 3 rows: P to end.

Bind off with Basic Bind Off method (page 17).

Weave ends in (page 19). Your scarf is complete!

Simple Hat

◉ ◉ ◉ ◉ ◉ │ **Head Size:** 18 to 20" (46 to 51cm) │ **Gauge:** 6 sts x 9 rows = 4" (10cm)

Knit a simple hat with a fat brim and eye-catching ribs. You'll be surprised how easy it is! Knit a few to give away as gifts during the holiday season.

Instructions:

Assemble 4 Zippy Looms + 4 Zippy Corners (20 pegs total). CO 20 pegs using E-Wrap Cast On (page 17). Prepare to work in the round.

Rnds 1–4: *K2, p2; rep from * to end of rnd.

Rnds 5–14: K to end of rnd.

Rnd 15–16: *K2, p2; rep from * to end of rnd.

Rnd 17: *K2, skip 2 pegs with yarn behind the peg; rep from * to the end of rnd.

Bind-off sts using Gather Bind Off method (page 19).

What's Needed:

Loom: 4 Zippy Looms + 4 Zippy Corners, 20 pegs total

Yarn: Approx 60 yds (55m) super-bulky or jumbo yarn. (Samples use Isaac Mizrahi CRAFT Lexington in Irving; and Loops & Threads, Artisan, discontinued.)

 or

Notions: Knitting tool, crochet hook, scissors.

Soft Smiles Hat

 | **Head Size:** Fits up to 21" (53cm) | **Gauge:** 6 sts x 8 rows = 4" (10cm)

Love a hat that hugs your head just right? This beanie has a distinctive ribbed pattern and no thick brim, so you can choose to wear it flat or rolled up. You'll be surprised how easy it is to knit up!

Instructions:

Assemble 6 Zippy Looms + 4 L connectors (24 pegs total). CO 24 pegs and prepare to work in the round.

Rnds 1–6: *K2, p2; rep from * to end.

Rnd 7: *K3, p1; rep from * to end.

Rnd 8: K to end.

Rep rnds 7–8 until item measures approx 7" (18cm) from cast-on edge.

Next rnd: *K2, p2; rep from * to end.

Cut a 20" (51cm) piece of yarn; remove all the k sts onto this piece of yarn. Cinch the first set of sts.

Cut another 20" (51cm) piece of yarn; remove the p sts onto this yarn and cinch the 2nd set of sts.

Weave ends in (page 9).

What's Needed:

Knitting Loom: 6 Zippy Looms + 4 "L" Connectors, 24 pegs total

Yarn: Approx 44 yds (40m) super-bulky or jumbo weight acrylic yarn. (Sample uses Knit Picks Tuff Puff in Flamingo.)

 or

Notions: Knitting tool, crochet hook, scissors.

Zippy Classic Hat and Scarf

 Head Size: Hat fits up to 22" (56cm) **Scarf Size:** Approx 86" (218cm)
Gauge: 6 sts x 8 rows = 4" (10cm)

This is a classic—you will love the way this hat and scarf set knits up so fast and fits so well. Make a set for yourself or as the perfect winter gift! With such a fast and simple project, you can have a set in all your favorite colors and yarns.

What's Needed:

Knitting Loom: 6 Zippy Looms + 4 Zippy Corners, 28 pegs total

Yarn: Approx 176 yds (161m) super-bulky or jumbo acrylic yarn. (Sample uses Knit Picks Tuff Puff in Silver.)

 or

Notions: Knitting tool, crochet hook, scissors.

Instructions:

Hat

Assemble 6 Zippy Looms + 4 Zippy Corners together (total 28 pegs). CO 28 sts and prepare to work in the round.

Rnds 1–6: *K2, p2; rep from * to end.

Rnd 7: K to end.

Rep rnd 7 until piece measures 7½" (19cm) from cast-on edge.

Next rnd: *K2, p2; rep from *.

Cut a 20" (51cm) piece of yarn; remove all the k sts onto this piece of yarn.

Cut another 20" (51cm) piece of yarn and remove all remaining loops onto it (all the p sts).

Cinch the first set of sts.

Cinch the 2nd set of sts.

Weave ends in (page 19).

Scarf

Set up a loom with 3 Zippy Looms. CO 10 sts; prepare to work a flat panel.

Row 1: *K2, p2; rep from * to last 2 sts, k2.

Rep row 1 until item measures approx 86" (218cm) from cast-on edge.

Bind off with Basic Bind Off method (page 17).

Weave all ends in (page 19).

Block lightly (page 9).

Blanket Jacket

😊 😊 😊 😊 😊 | **Size:** Approx 50 x 35" (127 x 89cm) | **Gauge:** 6 sts x 10 rows = 4" (10cm)

There's nothing as great, when the weather starts getting chilly, as a cozy blanket shawl. This stylish design can be worn at home watching a movie, or worn out when you go shopping. Cozy and warm!

What's Needed:

Knitting Loom: 10 Zippy Looms + 4 Zippy Corners, 44 pegs total

Yarn: Approx 370 yds (338m) super-bulky or jumbo acrylic yarn. (Sample uses Patons Cobbles in Dreamy.)

 or

Notions: Knitting tool, tapestry needle, crochet hook, scissors.

Instructions:

Assemble 10 Zippy Looms + 4 Zippy Corners in a rectangle (44 pegs total). CO 43 sts; prepare to work a flat panel.

Rows 1, 3, 5, 7: *K1, p1; rep from * to last st, k1.

Rows 2, 4, 6, 8: *P1, k1; rep from * to last st, p1.

Row 9: K1, p1, k1, p1, k to last 4 sts, p1, k1, p1, k1.

Row 10: P1, k1, p1, k to last 3 sts, p1, k1, p1.

Rep rows 9–10 until panel measures approx 50" (127cm) from cast-on edge.

Rep rows 1–8.

Bind off with Basic Bind Off method (page 17).

Weave ends in (page 19).

Block lightly (page 9).

ASSEMBLY

1 Lay the item on a flat surface, with the wrong side facing up. The cast-on edge should be at the bottom, and the bind-off edge should be at the top.

Bind off edge
Cast on edge

2 Find the panel's mid-point. Fold down the bind-off edge to the mid-point. Fold up the cast-on edge to the panel's mid-point.

Bind off edge
Fold half way
Cast on edge

Blanket Jacket

3 Using tapestry needle and yarn, mattress-stitch (page 19) about 8" (20cm) at each end where the top and the bottom sections meet. Weave ends in. Block lightly again, if necessary.

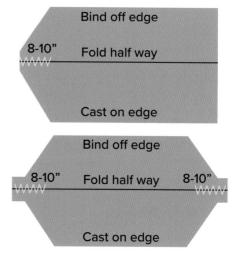

Sweet Savannah Blanket

☺☺☺☺☺ | **Size:** 36 x 48" (91 x 122cm) | **Gauge:** 5½ sts x 10 rows = 4" (10cm)

How snuggly is this for sitting by the fire? How about laying on your full-size bed? Wherever you use it, this beautiful checkerboard blanket will be a favorite.

What's Needed:

Knitting Loom: 12 Zippy Looms + 4 Zippy Corners, 52 pegs total

Yarn: Approx 468 yds (428m) super-bulky or jumbo acrylic yarn. (Sample uses Lion Brand Color Clouds in Fortune Teller Teal.)

Notions: Knitting tool, crochet hook, scissors.

Instructions:

Assemble 12 Zippy Looms + 4 Zippy Corners in a rectangle (52 pegs total). CO 51 sts; prepare to work a flat panel.

Row 1, 3, 5, 7: K to end of row.

Row 2, 4, 6, 8: P to end of row.

Row 9: K3, [p1, k8]5x, k3. (If using chart, begin here; see page 45.)

Row 10: P3, [k7, p2]5x, p3.

Row 11: K3, [p3, k6]5x, k3.

Row 12: P3 [k5, p4]5x, p3.

Row 13: K3 [p5, k4]5x, k3.

Row 14: P3, [k3, p6]5x, p3.

Row 15: K3, [p7, k2]5x, k3.

Row 16: P3, [k1, p8]5x, p3.

Row 17: K3, [k8, p1]5x, k3.

Row 18: P3, [p2, k7]5x, p3.

Row 19: K3, [k6, p3]5x, k3.

Row 20: P3, [p4, k5]5x, p3.

Row 21: K3, [k4, p5]5x, k3.

Row 22: P3, [p6, k3]5x, p3.

Row 23: K3, [k2, p7]5x, k3.

Row 24: P3, [p8, k1]5x, p3.

Rep rows 9–24 until panel measures approx 45" (114cm) from cast-on edge.

Rep rows 1–8.

Bind off with Basic Bind Off method (page 17).

Weave ends in (page 19).

Block lightly (page 9).

Sweet Savannah Blanket

Instructions *(continued)*

PENNANTS CHART

	9	8	7	6	5	4	3	2	1	
24	●	●	●	●	●	●	●	●		
		●	●	●	●	●	●	●		23
22	●	●	●	●	●	●				
		●	●	●	●	●				21
20	●	●	●	●						
		●	●	●						19
18	●	●								
	●									17
16		●	●	●	●	●	●	●	●	
			●	●	●	●	●	●	●	15
14				●	●	●	●	●	●	
					●	●	●	●	●	13
12						●	●	●	●	
							●	●	●	11
10								●	●	
									●	9

LEGEND:

● = purl

☐ = knit

Cozy Rug

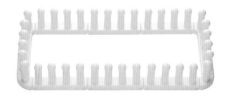

Approx size: 38 x 44" (97 x 112cm), not including tassels

No more chilly feet from unforgiving tile and wood floors—simply whip up a throw rug to warm your feet and give your floors a pop of color. This rug is loaded with texture to add to your home décor.

What's Needed:

Knitting Loom: 8 Zippy Looms + 4 Zippy Corners, 36 pegs total

Yarn: Approx 330 yds (302m) super-bulky or jumbo acrylic yarn. (Sample uses Premier Yarns Couture Jazz in Denim.)

Notions: Knitting tool, crochet hook, scissors.

Instructions:

Assemble 8 Zippy Looms + 4 Zippy Corners (36 pegs total). CO 36 sts; prepare to work a flat panel.

Row 1: E-wrap knit to end.

Row 2: P to end.

Rep rows 1–2 until panel measures approx 44" (112cm) from cast-on edge.

Tassels

Cut 108 pieces of yarn, each 14" (36cm) in length, to create the tassels. Each tassel will have 3 strands; you will use 54 yarn pieces on the cast-on edge and 54 on the bind-off edge.

1 Use 3 strands of yarn for one fringe. Fold in half, forming a small loop at one edge, making sure the ends are even in length.

2 Use crochet hook and draw the loop through the single crochet st where you are attaching the fringe.

3 Now catch the loose ends of the yarn strand through the loop (thus creating the loop).

4 Tighten the knot by pulling gently on the fringe ends with your hand and holding the knot with the other hand.

5 Trim the ends if necessary to make all the tassels/fringes the same length.

6 Attach half of the tassels to the cast-on edge and half to the bind-off edge.

Little Apple Hat

○●○○○ | **Size:** 14" diameter x 7" high (36 x 18cm) | **Gauge:** 8 sts x 10 rows = 4" (10cm)

This cute beanie is sure to please your someone special. It features a thin spiral winding around from the base to the crown—a fast, creative knit.

Instructions:

Assemble 4 Zippy Looms + 4 Zippy Corners (20 pegs total). CO 20 sts and prepare to work in the round.

Rnds 1–6: *K2, p2; rep from *.

Rnd 7: *K3, p1, rep from *.

Rnd 8: K2, p1, *k3, p1, rep from * to last st, k1.

Rnd 9: K1, p1, *k3, p1, rep from * to last 2 sts, k2.

Rnd 10: *P1, k3, rep from *.

Rep rnds 7–10 until hat measures approx 6 ½" (17cm) from cast-on edge.

Next rnd: *K2, p2; rep from * to end.

Cut 2 pieces of yarn that are each approx 20" (51cm) long.

Using tapestry needle and one of the lengths of yarn, remove all the k sts onto this piece of yarn.

Rep with the 2nd piece of yarn and remaining sts (all the p sts).

Cinch the first set of sts; secure knot with a square knot.

Cinch the 2nd set of sts and secure with a square knot.

Weave ends in (page 19).

Block lightly, if needed (page 9).

What's Needed:

Knitting loom: 4 Zippy Looms + 4 Zippy Corners, 20 pegs total

Yarn: Approx 35 yds (32m) super-bulky or jumbo acrylic blend yarn. (Samples uses Knit Picks Mighty Stitch Super Bulky in Serrano.)

 or

Notions: Knitting tool, crochet hook, scissors.

Magical Stitch Blanket

😊 😊 😊 😊 😊 | **Size:** 36 x 48" (91 x 122cm) | **Gauge:** 5½ sts x 10 rows = 4" (10cm)

A procession of intriguing stitch textures makes this blanket not only warm and cuddly, but also lends a great visual with a little bit of magic. Select four colors that you like together and get started!

What's Needed:

Knitting Loom: 12 Zippy Looms + 4 Zippy Corners, 52 pegs total

Yarn: Approx 520 yds (476m) total super-bulky or jumbo acrylic and wool blend yarn: gray (A), 161 yds (147m); pink (B), 138 yds (126m); white (C), 138 yds (126m); purple (D), 80½ yds (74m). (Sample uses Red Heart Grande in Foggy [A], 3½ skeins; Nectar [B], 3 skeins; Aran [C], 3 skeins; and Currant [D], 1¾ skeins.)

 or

Notions: Knitting tool, crochet hook, scissors.

Instructions:

Assemble knitting loom in a rectangular configuration using 12 Zippy Looms + 4 Corners (52 pegs total). Blanket is worked in color sections and requires no sewing.

Using CA (gray), CO 52 sts; prepare to work a flat panel.

Section 1
Row 1: K to end of row.

Row 2: P to end of row.

Rep rows 1–2 until section measures 7" (18cm) in length. (Sample used 18 rows.)

Cut CA (gray), join CB (pink).

Section 2
Using CB (pink):

Row 1: K to end of row.

Row 2: P4, k to last 4 sts, p4.

Rep rows 1–2 until section measures 7" (18cm) in length. (Sample used 18 rows.)

Cut CB (pink), join CC (white).

Section 3
Using CC (white):

Row 1: K4, *k1, p1; rep from * to last 4 sts, k4.

Row 2: P4, *k1, p1; rep from * to last 4 sts, p4.

Rep rows 1–2 until section measures 7" (18cm) in length. (Sample used 18 rows.)

Cut CC (white), join CD (purple).

Section 4
Using CD (purple):

Row 1: K4, [k4, p4] 5x, k8.

Row 2: P4, k4, [p4, k4] 5x, p4.

Row 3: Rep row 1.

Row 4: Rep row 2.

Row 5: K4 [p4, k4] 5x, p4, k4.

Row 6: P8, [k4, p4] 5x, p4.

Row 7: Rep row 5.

Row 8: Rep row 6.

Rep rows 1–8.

Cut CD (purple), join CC (white).

Rep section 3.

Cut CC (white), join CB (pink).

Rep section 2.

Cut CB (pink), join CA (gray).

Rep section 1.

Bind off using Basic Bind Off method (page 17).

Weave ends in (page 19).

Block lightly (page 9).

Plum Garden Wrap

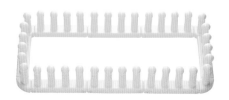

😊😊😊🙂🙂 | **Approx size:** 27 x 75" (69 x 191cm) | **Gauge:** 8 sts x 10 rows = 4" (10cm)

Wrap yourself in luxury; select yarn with soft pastels for a reminder of spring gardens.

Instructions:

Assemble knitting loom in a rectangular configuration using 8 Zippy Looms + 4 Zippy Corners (36 pegs total). CO 36 sts; prepare to work a flat panel.

Row 1, 3, 5: K to end.

Row 2, 4, 6: P to end.

Row 7: K to end.

Row 8: P2, k2, [p2, k3]6x, p2.

Row 9: K2, [k2, LT, k1]6x, k to end.

Row 10: P2, k2, [p1, k1, p1, k2]6x, p2.

Row 11: K2, [k3, LT]6x, k4.

Row 12: P2, k2 [k1, p2, k2]6x, p2.

Row 13: K to end.

Row 14: P2, k2, [k1, p2, k2]6x, p2.

Row 15: K2, [k3, RT]6x, k4.

Row 16: P2, k2, [p1, k1, p1, k2]6x, p2.

Row 17: K2, [k2, RT, k1]6x, k4.

Row 18: P2, k2, [p2, k3]6x, p2.

Rep rows 7–18 until panel measures 72" (183cm) from cast-on edge.

Rep rows 1–6.

Bind off with Basic Bind Off method (page 17).

Weave ends in (page 19).

Block lightly (page 9).

PLUM GARDEN WRAP CHART FOR ROWS 8 TO 18

	7	6	5	4	3	2	1	
18			•	•				
				╳				17
16			•		•			
			╳	╳				15
14				•	•			
								13
12				•	•			
			╳	╳				11
10			•		•			
				╳	╳			9
8			•	•				
								7

LEGEND:

☐ = knit   ╳╳ = Left Twist

• = purl   ╳╳ = Right Twist

What's Needed:

Knitting Loom: 8 Zippy Looms + 4 Zippy Corners, 36 pegs total

Yarn: Approx 440 yds (402m) super-bulky or jumbo acrylic blend yarn. (Sample uses Lion Brand Color Clouds in Summer Rain.)

 or

Notions: Knitting tool, tapestry needle, crochet hook, scissors.

Special Stitches You'll Need

LEFT TWIST (LT)

Skip peg 1 with yarn behind the peg. Knit peg 2. Remove loop from peg 2 and hold it. Take yarn to the front of peg 1 and knit peg 1. Remove loop from peg 1 and place it on peg 2. Place the loop that you are holding on peg 1.

RIGHT TWIST (RT)

Remove loop from peg 1, place it on a cable needle, and place it to the center of the knitting loom. Knit peg 2. Move loop from peg 2 and place it on peg 1. Place the loop from the cable needle on peg 2. Knit peg 2.

Braided Pillow

☺ ☺ ☺ ☺ ☺ | **Size:** 12 x 12" (31 x 31cm) | **Gauge:** 7 sts x 10 rows = 4" (10cm)

Craft a multitude of these elegant braided pillows to cover your sofa with softness. Easy to knit and makes a great set with the foot stool.

Instructions:

Assemble 4 Zippy Looms + 4 Zippy Corners (20 pegs total). CO 20 sts; prepare to work a flat panel.

Row 1, 3, 5: P to end.

Row 2, 4, 6: K to end.

Row 7: P3, BO 5, p to end.

Row 8: K12, CO 5, k to end.

Row 9: P to end.

Row 10: K to end.

Rep rows 7–10, 12 more times.

Braiding
See instructions on performing the braid in the sidebar on page 56.

Finishing
BO with Basic Bind Off method (page 17).

Weave ends in (page 19).

Block lightly (page 9).

Seaming
Fold horizontally and mattress-stitch (page 19) seam down the left and right sides, leaving the top open. Insert pillow form and continue seaming.

What's Needed:

Knitting Loom: 4 Zippy Looms + 4 Zippy Corners, 20 pegs total

Yarn: Approx 160 yds (146m) super-bulky or jumbo merino wool yarn. (Sample uses Knit Picks Tuff Puff in Silver.)

 or

Notions: Knitting tool, tapestry needle, 12 x 12" (31 x 31cm) pillow form, crochet hook, scissors.

Braided Pillow

Braiding

1 Lay the knitting out flat.

2 Hold the bottommost ladder (cast-on edge) and twist it clockwise.

3 Twist until a loop is formed.

4 Grab the next top ladder and pass it through the opening.

5 Grab the next ladder through the eyelet opening.

6 Continue in this manner until you reach the last ladder.

Cable Cowl and Wristers

☺ ☺ ☺ ☺ ☺ | **Size:** 12 x 13" (30 x 33cm) | **Gauge:** 7 sts x 10 rows = 4" (10cm)

Convert any shirt into a turtleneck with this cozy cowl. The stylish wristers make it easy to keep your fingers and wrists warm. Coordinate with style! See pages 15–16 for complete cable instructions with illustrations.

What's Needed:

Knitting Loom: 8 Zippy Looms + 4 Zippy Corners, 36 pegs total

Yarn: Approx 180 yds (165m) super-bulky or jumbo yarn. (Sample uses Malabrigo Rasta in Plomo.)

Notions: Knitting tool, crochet hook, scissors, cable needle.

Special Stitches You'll Need

SKIP WITH YARN TO BACK (SL1WYB)
Skip 1 peg with yarn toward the back of the peg.

CABLE 1 OVER 2 LEFT (C1 OVER 2 LEFT)
Skip peg 1 with yarn behind peg; knit peg 2 and peg 3. Place loop from peg 2 and peg 3 on cable needle; hold cable needle to the center of the knitting loom. Take working yarn to the front of peg 1. Knit peg 1. Move loop from peg 1 to peg 3. Place loops from cable needle on peg 1 and peg 2. Gently tug on the loop on peg 2, then on the loop on peg 3—this removes yarn slack from the sts.

CABLE 1 OVER 2 RIGHT (C1 OVER 2 RIGHT)
Place loops from peg 1 and peg 2 on cable needle; hold cable needle to the center of the knitting loom. Knit peg 3. Place loop from peg 3 on peg 1. Place sts from cable needle on peg 2 and peg 3. Knit peg 2, then knit peg 3. Gently tug on the loop on peg 2, then on the loop on peg 3—this removes yarn slack from the sts.

Cable Cowl and Wristers

Instructions:

Cowl

Assemble 8 Zippy Looms + 4 Zippy Corners (36 pegs total). CO 36 sts; prepare to work in the round.

Rnds 1–6: K2, p2, k3, p2, k to end.

Rnds 7–8: K2, p2, k2, sl1wyb, p2, k to end.

Rnd 9: K2, p2, c1 over 2 left, p2, k to end (see cable section on page 57).

Rnd 10: K2, p2, k3, p2, k to end.

Rep rnds 7–10, 4 more times.

Rep rnds 1–6.

Bind off with Basic Bind Off method (page 17).

Weave ends in (page 19).

Block lightly (page 9).

Right Hand Wrister

CO 15 sts; prepare to work a flat panel.

Row 1, 3, 5: K6, p2, k3, p2, k2.

Row 2, 4, 6: K2, p2, k3, p2, k6.

Row 7: K6, p2, sl1wyb, k2, p2, k2.

Row 8: K2, p2, k2, sl1wyb, p2, k6.

Row 9: K6, p2, c1 over 2 left, p2, k2.

Row 10: K2, p2, k3, p2, k6.

Rep rows 7–10, 2 more times.

Next row: K6, p2, k3, p2, k2.

Next row: K2, p2, k3, p2, k6.

Bind off with Basic Bind Off method (page 17).

Weave ends in (page 19).

Block lightly (page 9).

SEAMING

Fold vertically and begin a mattress stitch seam (page 19) from the cast-on edge up the side, stopping about 3" (8cm) from the bind-off edge. Begin mattress stitching at the bind-off edge and seam down about 1" (3cm), thus leaving an opening for the thumb.

Left Hand Wrister

CO 15 sts; prepare to work a flat panel.

Row 1, 3, 5: K2, p2, k3, p2, k6.

Row 2, 4, 6: K6, p2, k3, p2, k2.

Row 7: K2, p2, k2, sl1wyb, p2, k6.

Row 8: K6, p2, sl1wyb, k2, p2, k2.

Row 9: K2, p2, c1 over 2 right, p2, k6.

Row 10: K6, p2, k3, p2, k2.

Rep rows 7–10, 2 more times.

Next row: K2, p2, k3, p2, k6.

Next row: K6, p2, k3, p2, k2.

Bind off with Basic Bind Off method (page 17).

Weave ends in (page 19).

Block lightly (page 9).

Follow Seaming at left.

Faux Cable Foot Stool

☺ ☺ ☺ ☺ ☺ | **Size:** See Pattern Notes | **Gauge:** 6 sts x 9½ rows = 4" (10cm)

Create a comfy addition to your living room or den with this unique foot stool. The faux cable design and rounded top will add a touch of warmth in any home. So attractive!

Pattern Notes:

As this is working with very large pegs, knit with a snug (yet not too tight) tension throughout. Using the U st for the k st will help achieve a fabric that is not too holey for your finished pouf.

Notes on Stuffing

The sample is stuffed with a round pillow at both the top and bottom, with a folded and rolled 60 x 70 x ½" (152 x 178 x 1cm) foam pad on end in the center. This creates a very firm foot pouf that will hold its shape even when sat upon. Alternatively, those tired, worn out linens, duvets, and pillows that may be lying around the house can also be used. Make sure all items have been laundered before using to stuff the pouf. A pretty good stack of sheets and blankets will be needed to get a firm pouf that will easily support weight.

Pouf Measurements

(**All measurements given are approximate. Once the item is stuffed firmly, measurements may vary.)

Before Stuffing: Circumference, approx 44½" (113cm); Diameter, approx 14" (36cm); Height, approx 14" (36cm).

After Stuffing: Circumference, approx 52" (132cm); Diameter, approx 16" (41cm); Height: approx. 16" (41cm).

What's Needed:

Knitting Loom: 5 Zippy Looms (or 4 Zippy Looms + 4 Zippy Corners), 20 pegs total

Yarn: Approx 330 yds (302m) super-bulky or jumbo wool yarn. (Sample uses Knit Picks Tuff Puff in Silver.)

6 SUPER BULKY   or   7 JUMBO

Notions: Knitting tool, 6.5mm crochet hook (for cast on and help with possible missed stitches, etc), scissors, wide-eye yarn needle, row counter, knitting pins, removable stitch markers or bits of scrap yarn, stuffing of choice (see Pattern Notes for more details).

Special Stitches You'll Need

SLIP 1 STITCH (S1)
Do not knit the peg; carry working yarn behind peg.

WRAP AND TURN (W&T)
Remove the loop from the peg and hold it. With working yarn, simply wrap around the peg, and then place the loop back on the peg.

Faux Cable Foot Stool

Top & Bottom Instructions (Make 2):

Connect 2 Zippy Looms together for a total of 8 pegs. CO to all 8 pegs.

Prepare to create a series of 8 short row wedges.

Row 1: S1, k1, W&T peg 3.

Row 2: K2 back to peg 1.

Row 3: S1, k2 (KO 2 over 1 on peg with 2 loops), W&T peg 4.

Row 4: K3 back to peg 1.

Row 5: S1, k3 (KO 2 over 1 on peg with 2 loops), W&T peg 5.

Row 6: K4 back to peg 1.

Row 7: S1, k4 (KO 2 over 1 on peg with 2 loops), W&T peg 6.

Row 8: K5 back to peg 1.

Row 9: S1, k5 (KO 2 over 1 on peg with 2 loops), W&T peg 7.

Row 10: K6 back to peg 1.

Row 11: S1, k6 (KO 2 over 1 on peg with 2 loops), W&T peg 8.

Row 12: K7 back to peg 1.

Row 13: S1, k7 (on 8th peg KO 2 sts over 1).

Row 14: S1, k7.

Rep rows 1–14 7 more times to create a total of 8 wedges—except on row 14 of 8th wedge.

Row 14 of 8th wedge: BO all sts. Leave a length of yarn in place for seaming.

Using yarn tail, seam up BO and CO edges, moving toward the center of circle. Gather the loose stitches at the inside of center and cinch tightly. Knot and trim.

To achieve a flat and uniform shape, block lightly (page 9).

Sides Instructions:

Connect 5 Zippy Looms together for a total of 20 pegs (alternatively, 4 Zippy Looms + 4 Zippy Corners could also be used). CO to 18 pegs to work as a flat panel.

Row 1
(Follow instructions for each peg below.)

Pegs 1–3: K.

CORD WITHIN ROW 1
Begin a 6-row, 2-peg I-cord on pegs 2–3:

❶ *Bring WY behind peg 3 and around to front of peg 2.

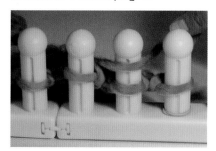